A SECRET HIT

A Secret Hit: 150 years of Max Stirner's
Der Einzige und sein Eigentum
isbn: 978-1-943687-30-5
First edition, November 2023.

Originally published as Ein heimlicher Hit: 150 Jahre Stirners "Einziger":
eine kurze Editionsgeschichte in 1994, © Bernd A. Laska.

Published by Underworld Amusements & Union of Egoists
Translated in 2023 by the Union of Egoists.
Edited and designed by Kevin I. Slaughter.
Copyediting by Alex Kies.

More information:
www.UnionOfEgoists.com
www.UnderworldAmusements.com

Stand Alone SA1280

Published as part of the Stand Alone series by the Union of Egoists. Stand
Alone is mixed medium and format journal produced at irregular intervals.
The focus is Egoism and the individuals associated with it.

A SECRET HIT

IN THE SECOND HALF OF OCTOBER IN THE YEAR 1844, a previously unknown author, Max Stirner, emerged with an extensive philosophical work, which he had given the peculiar title *Der Einzige und sein Eigentum* (The Ego and His Own). Stirner polemicizes throughout against contemporary authors, primarily against Bruno Bauer and Ludwig Feuerbach, the leading minds of the so-called Young Hegelians, who were the first in Germany to espouse an explicitly atheist standpoint. Stirner, however, does not attack them, as most of his contemporaries did, because of their atheism, but rather because they did not represent it consistently enough. *Der Einzige* caused a scandalous stir for a short time, but disappeared completely from public discourse two to three years later.

The revolution of March 1848, which was soon followed by a longer period of reaction, was the historical turning point that ended the radical Young Hegelian discussions altogether. The Young Hegelian movement was then categorically relegated to the footnotes of the history of ideas as a "symptom of decay of the Hegelian school." Stirner's *Der Einzige*, although clearly a work (also) against Young Hegelianism, was mostly attributed to it—as its self-destructive conclusion. The ideological classification of Young Hegelianism as an episode of confusion and decay has not been fundamentally revised to this day. It is said that only one significant thinker emerged from that chaotic time: Karl Marx.

Against this roughly sketched background, it seems particularly astonishing Stirner's *Der Einzige* has had an extraordinary, highly interesting, and in a non-trivial sense singular 150 years of existence, a history of impact still not considered to be finished today. Although this work, like the entire Young Hegelian literature, was quickly forgotten, it was rediscovered after a long time as the only contribution to that *Vormärz* (pre-March)[1] discussion, and then rediscovered again after being forgotten once more.

The first so-called Stirner Renaissance began in the 1890s, after *Der Einzige* had been lost for nearly half a century. At that time, Stirner was seen as surprisingly radical and daring, but ultimately only a curiosity and too vulgar precursor to Nietzsche and/or a forerunner of contemporary anarchists—although neither

....

1   *Vormärz* was a period in the history of Germany preceding the 1848 March Revolution in the states of the German Confederation.—UoE.

Nietzscheans nor anarchists wanted to accept him as their predecessor. Although many authors were somehow fascinated by Stirner, as can be seen in his works and the majority of writings about him at the time, there was no one who really knew how to appreciate Stirner as an independent thinker, so he eventually fell into obscurity.

The second Renaissance of the supposed Young Hegelian *Der Einzige* occurred in the 1960s, after another half century of being overshadowed. At this time, Stirner was primarily seen as a seductive ideologist whom Karl Marx had already unmasked once and for all as a pseudo-radical, frenzied *petit-bourgeois*, and/or as an early existential philosopher—although Marx never published this "unmasking" of Stirner and no authentic existential philosopher accepted Stirner as his predecessor. Stirner was still not recognized as an independent thinker. Presentations of philosophy and intellectual history still only mention him as mostly a footnote to Marx or Nietzsche.

This unanimous marginalization of Stirner is in striking contrast to the fact of the sales success of his *Der Einzige*—which is not to be evaluated from a commercial point of view here. It is already astonishing that *Der Einzige*, this voluminous and cumbersome text, considered eccentric in the frame of discussion, was even rediscovered. Even more surprising, however, is during its two Renaissances (roughly beginning 1893 and 1968), it reached sales figures that are exceptionally high for books of this genre. As will be shown later, it was a veritable bookselling "hit" twice over decades—although not really perceived as such, rather as a "secret hit."

One explanation for the inconspicuous popularity of *Der Einzige und sein Eigentum* which is occasionally put forward assumes the infamous book, which is thought to justify vulgar egoism, was particularly appreciated by those numerous petit-bourgeois existences who, after their mundane daily business, seek solace in intellectually stimulating and intricate reading material for enlightenment. It is posited that it is because *Der Einzige und sein Eigentum* is well-suited to giving their banal lives and practices a philosophically resonant sense.

This may well be one aspect under which the "success" of *Der Einzige* is partly explicable; however, another aspect appears to be more interesting, especially for an understanding of Stirner's role in the history of ideas.

Stirner's *Der Einzige* was not only a bookseller's hit, but also—if one understands the term in the proper sense as a blow or hit—an intellectual "hit," and a secret one at that. Because with its first appearance, it had a profound impact on its most important addressees (Feuerbach, Ruge, Engels, and, above all, Marx), which they carefully concealed from the public. How deeply these irritations affected each individual case is therefore hardly discernible from the writings that were published in reaction to *Der Einzige*, but all the more apparent from private, sometimes posthumously published testimonies.

Remarkably, *Der Einzige und sein Eigentum* continued to have this effect even later, up to our time. The list of thinkers who felt themselves "hit" by Stirner in an extraordinary way and therefore also dealt with him "secretly" is an impressive series of prominent names: from Karl Marx (who concealed the decisive role of *Der Einzige* in the conception of historical materialism) to Friedrich Nietzsche (who almost completely erased all traces of his knowledge of *Der Einzige*) and Carl Schmitt (who had to struggle with Stirner, whom he had suppressed for forty years, only in the desperation of solitary confinement) to Jürgen Habermas (who, as a young man, tried to defend himself against the "absurdity of Stirner's madness" with his own madness, but then suppressed Stirner so thoroughly that he has not even mentioned him to this day—not even in his relevant specialized works, such as on the Young Hegelians, on the emergence of historical materialism).[2]

....

2   Regarding Karl Marx: Wolfgang Essbach: *"Die Bedeutung Max Stirners für die Genese des historischen Materialismus"* (The Significance of Max Stirner for the Genesis of Historical Materialism). Dissertation, University of Göttingen, 1978; expanded as a book entitled: *Gegenzüge. Der Materialismus des Selbst und seine Ausgren zung*

As interesting as the fact that the *Einzige* was a veritable intellectual "hit" for a considerable number—the above list is by no means complete—of outstanding thinkers, mostly in their younger years, the other fact is of course equally interesting: that they processed, overcame, and kept as a private matter the way in which they rejected him; that they only mastered the intellectual challenge that they initially only characterized with superlatives "secretly" and not through an argumentative, publicly presentable parade; that they suppressed the problematic issues raised by Stirner and created a counter-philosophy whose cause they falsified or left in the dark. More or less, they probably all felt that "seductive power" of *Der Einzige*, which, for example, Edmund Husserl did

aus dem Marxismus (Counter-Movements. The Materialism of the Self and its Exclusion from Marxism). Frankfurt: Materialis-Verlag, 1982.

Regarding Friedrich Nietzsche: Bernd A. Laska: *"Neues Licht auf die Stirner Nietzsche-Frage"* (New Light on the Stirner-Nietzsche Question). Lecture at the First Dortmund Nietzsche Colloquium on July 5, 1991. Published in *Stirner-Studien*, No. 4.

Regarding Carl Schmitt: Bernd A. Laska: *"'Katechon' und 'Anarch': Carl Schmitts und Ernst Jüngers Reaktionen auf Stirner.* ("'Katechon' and 'Anarch': Carl Schmitt's and Ernst Jünger's Reactions to Stirner"). Lecture at the Congress "Max Stirner and Modern Individualism", Naples (Italy), November 10–12, 1994. An expanded version was published in 1997 in *Stirner-Studien*, No. 3.

Regarding Hagen Habermas, see: ibid.: *"Das Absolute und die Geschichte"* (The Absolute and History). Dissertation, University of Bonn, 1954, pp. 23–34.

not even want to warn against, because it makes "philosophical beginners" curious and endangered.[3]

Out of the hordes of those who later dealt in detail with the intellectual development of those influential thinkers, very few paid closer attention to the important biographical points highlighted here. Almost all of them practiced a secondary avoidance of Stirner, *i.e.* the uncritical reproduction of the (primary) avoidance of the examined authors, without perceiving it as such (which can be impressively demonstrated, especially in the research on Marx[4]). Many of them, especially the Marx and Nietzsche researchers, may have occasionally used *Der Einzige*; they probably constitute, alongside the aforementioned "petty bourgeois," the second large contingent of those who have caused the commercial success of the book.

....

3   Husserl does not mention Stirner in his published works. However, see his manuscript Vol. 128, p. 118 in the Husserl Archive in Leuven, Belgium.

4   The most daring attempt so far has been made by Wolfgang Essbach, op. cit. In the preface to his book, he wrote: "*Wäre nicht geschrieben worden, wenn ich den etablierten wissenschaftlichen und politischen Auffassungen hätte trauen können, und es würde nicht publiziert sein, wenn es sich bloss urn ein akribisches Ausfüllen von Forschungslücken in einem Spezialgebiet handelte*" (This would not have been written if I had trusted established scientific and political views, and it would not be published if it were only an exhaustive exploration of research gaps in a specialized field). He soon retreated from this topic and pursued an academic career.

The social impact (*Wirkungsgeschichte*) and publishing history (*Editionsgeschichte*) of a work or book, as this introductory sketch shows—whether one follows its unorthodox view of reception or not—are always closely linked.[5] When the fate of books is discussed, usually only the former is meant, for the latter is usually a rather dry, bibliographical matter. In the case of Stirner's *Der Einzige*, however, the history of its various editions is also exceptional and exciting. If this is described here, as far as possible separated and isolated, it is also done with the intention of shedding new light on the reception history by uncovering some of the effective motives in it.

Who was this author who left behind only this one book, this *homo unius libri*? Max Stirner is the pseudonym for Johann Caspar Schmidt. Schmidt, who was born in

5   See also Bernd A. Laska: *"Der schwierige Stirner"* (The Difficult Stirner). In: Wolfram Beyer (ed.): *Anarchisten. Zur Aktualität anarchistischer Klassiker.* (Anarchists: On the Topicality of Anarchist Classics). Berlin: Oppo-Verlag, 1993, pp. 9–25; as well as ibid.: *Ein dauerhafter Dissident. 150 Jahre Stirners. Eine kurze Wirkungsgeschichte.* (A Lasting Dissident: 150 Years of Stirner's *Der Einzige*: A Brief History of its Impact.). Nuremberg: LSR-Verlag, 1996 (Stirner-Studien, No. 2). Ibid.: "Anarchismus, individualistischer" (Individualistic Anarchism) and "Stirner" in: Hans Jürgen Degen (ed.): *Lexikon der Anarchie* (Lexicon of Anarchy). Bösdorf: Verlag Schwarzer Nachtschatten, 1993.

1806 in the Franconian town of Bayreuth.[6] His parents were simple people but had enabled their only child to obtain a university degree. In 1826, Schmidt went to the University of Berlin, where he studied under, among others, Hegel and Schleiermacher. However, he abandoned his studies after just four semesters and left Berlin. Five years later, in 1833, he returned and completed two more semesters, apparently only to fulfill the minimum requirements for teaching. At the age of 33, in 1839, Schmidt finally took his first paid job as a teacher at a girls' school in Berlin, which he left five years later, shortly before the publication of *Der Einzige*.

From mid-1841, Schmidt associated with the Berlin "*Freien*" (The Free), a loose scene of oppositional writers and journalists around the former Hegelian nd theologian Bruno Bauer. At that time, Schmidt began to work as a journalist and occasionally signed his articles with "Stirner." The only reasonably authentic characterization of Schmidt comes from this time. Friedrich Engels and Edgar Bauer, both "*Freie*," depict Stirner in a burlesque "heroic poem" that parodies the antics of this group and calls out to his friends: "*Den Willen bindet ihr, ihr wagt's*

....

6 The little that is known about him today was collected by the German poet John Henry Mackay in the early 1900s. See: ibid: *Max Stirner. Sein Leben und sein Werk* (Max Stirner. His Life and His Work). First edition, 1898; Second, expanded edition, 1910; Third, further expanded edition, 1914; reprint of the Third edition. Freiburg: Mackay Society, 1977.

und nennt euch frei / Wie seid ihr eingelebt noch in die Sklaverei!" (You bind the will, you dare and call your-selves free / How deeply you are still enmeshed in slav-ery!).[7] Not us, but you! You and—I. The sketch shows Stirner as a dissident even among dissidents, which is how he proved himself in *Der Einzige*. According to ev-erything that has been passed down about him, Stirner felt that he did not really belong to any group, not even the Young Hegelians or the "*Freie.*"

The leading philosophical minds of the Young Hegelians, Ludwig Feuerbach and Bruno Bauer, wanted to revive the atheistic enlightenment of the 18th century, which had been suppressed in France and had not even been given a chance to take root against the prevailing theologizing enlightenment in Germany. Stirner certain-ly agreed with them on this, but he saw that they had stopped halfway and neglected the "becoming practical" of philosophy: "The beyond outside us is indeed swept away, and the great undertaking of the Enlightenment accomplished; but the beyond in us calls us to renewed heavenly storms."[8] These words, in their shortened form,

---

7   Friedrich Engels: *The Insolently Threatened Yet Miraculously Rescued Bible: Or, The Triumph of Faith.* Canto III. In: Marx-Engels Werke, Supplementary Volume, Part Two. Berlin): Dietz, 1967, pp. 283–316 (304).

8   Max Stirner: *Der Einzige und sein Eigentum.* Stuttgart: Reclam 1972. p.170 (This is a citation for the specific edition of Stirner's book.)

describe Stirner's program, his vision, which *Der Einzige* was to be only the beginning. Since what Stirner described as the "beyond in us" has essentially persisted to this day, the impetus of *Der Einzige* can still be considered current. Stirner mocked Feuerbach and Bauer, the most radical thinkers of their time, as "pious atheists," but they and their followers were, despite being his opponents, the only ones who could have followed his arguments. *Der Einzige* mainly impacted them, and considerably, even leading to far-reaching consequences as seen in the case of Feuerbachian Karl Marx. However, for reasons still largely unexplored, Stirner's influence remained largely unknown.[9] The public discussion of the *Der Einzige*, to which Stirner had responded,[10] was superficial and revealed nothing of the "secret hit" described above. Stirner quickly became an "unperson"; there was no one willing to take up his position.

After the discussion about his work had died down, Stirner's life was marked by increasing external difficulties. His few later literary works are hardly worth mentioning. He died in 1856.

....

9   The details of Marx's reaction to Stirner are captured in Wolfgang Essbach (op. cit), although their interpretation remains within the conventional framework.

10   Max Stirner: *Rezensenten Stirners* (Stirner's Critics), in: ibid.: Parerga, Kritiken, Repliken (Parerga, Kritiken, Repliken), edited by Bernd A. Laska. Nürnberg: LSR-Verlag, 1986, pp. 147–205.

The first edition of the *Der Einzige*, which was delivered starting at the end of October 1844, bears the year 1845 in the imprint. The publisher was Otto Wigand in Leipzig, a politically engaged and courageous bookseller who published works by Bruno Bauer, Ludwig Feuerbach, and a number of other oppositional authors (Friedrich Engels, Arnold Ruge, Georg Friedrich Daumer, Richard Wagner) alongside commercially successful literature.[11]

At that time, in comparatively liberal Saxony, a book was exempt from prior censorship approval if it had at least 20 sheets, i.e., 320 pages, in length. Stirner did not expect his text to pass censorship and therefore wrote it initially with that page count in mind. When the manuscript grew even larger, it was probably because in the spring and summer of 1844, when he had already considered it finished, he added a series of fragments that took into account the latest state of the Young Hegelian discussion.[12]

Although the printing of *Der Einzige*, as it was not

---

11 See Inge Kiesshauer: "Otto Friedrich Wigand" (1795–1870). In: *Leipziger Jahrbuch zur Buchgeschichte* (Leipzig Annual for the Study of the History of the Book), No. 1 (1991), pp. 155–188.

12 See Stirner's remarks in: *Der Einzige...*, ibid., p. 159, 250 (This is also a citation for a specific edition of Stirner's book.)

subject to prior censorship, did not pose any problems, the distribution of the book was severely affected by subsequent censorship. Wigand had to submit a printed copy to the censorship authority at the beginning of the delivery process. *Der Einzige* was promptly banned, with the rationale that "*darin nicht allein Gott, Christus, die Kirche und die Religion überhaupt auf das Leichtfertigste gelästert, sondern auch alle sociale Verfassung, Staat und Regierung als etwas, das schlechthin nicht länger existiren dürfe, bezeichnet, die Lüge, der Meineid, Betrug, Mord und Selbstmord gerechtfertigt und das Recht des Eigenthums geleugnet wird.*" (not only God, Christ, the Church, and religion in general were blasphemed in it, but also all social structures, state and government were described as something that could no longer exist, and lying, perjury, fraud, murder, and suicide were justified, and the right to property was denied). However, the Saxon Minister of the Interior, the higher authority to whom Wigand appealed, lifted this ban a few days later. Although he confirmed the censor's characterization, he believed that the book would not cause any harm: "Ja die Schrift liest sich grossen theils sogar wie Ironie und eine schlagende Selbstwider legung..." (In fact, much of the writing is read as irony and a convincing self-refutation).[13]

....

13 Bert Andréas / Wolfgang Mönke: "Neue Daten zur 'Deutschen Ideologie'" (New Data on "The German Ideology"). In: *Archiv für*

The occasional assumption among readers that Stirner did not take the theses of his *Der Einzige*—or at least the "worst" ones—seriously, may partly stem from a (superficial) interpretation of the dedication that catches the reader's eye first, which is rather peculiar for a philosophical book: *"Meinem Liebchen Marie Dähnhardt"* (To my darling Marie Dähnhardt).—Marie Dähnhardt was Stirner's wife's maiden name. Stirner had met her among the *"Freie"* and had been married to her for almost a year by the time he finished the manuscript. According to *Rezensenten Stirners*,[14] Marie Dähnhardt had turned from a young girl who smoked cigars and drank with the *"Freie"* into a "quarrelsome wife". Therefore, the dedication does not seem to have been a mere joke that many readers apparently took it to be, nor just a whimsical jab at the scholarly philosophers' seriousness, but rather a bitter-ironic commentary on women's (and men's) emancipation, whose profound problematicity Stirner saw more clearly than his overly optimistic, enlightened contemporaries. Perhaps Stirner also intended to mislead the censorship authorities, as he apparently succeeded in doing in some cases, according to the above-quoted judgment.

Sozialgeschichte (Archive for Social History), 8 (1968), pp. 5–15 (18f, footnote 21).

14   "Szeliga." This remark is referred to by Stirner in: *Rezensenten Stirners*, op. cit., p. 156.

The censorship practice towards *Der Einzige* fluctuated from prohibition to lifting of the ban and then to re-prohibition in the other German states. While the book's content was universally condemned, not every authority considered a ban appropriate. Wigand, for one, was such a seasoned man in the business of banned books that it was no problem for him to ensure *Der Einzige* reached its most important addressees on time, in some cases even before its official release (in the form of posting sheets). The lack of more precise data on the first edition's print run and the losses due to seizures is therefore irrelevant here. The silencing of the discussion about *Der Einzige* in 1847 was primarily due to the social impacts mentioned earlier, and these are more interesting and important than the censorious restrictions on book trade.

Over the following four decades, *Der Einzige* was only rarely mentioned. It is therefore difficult to estimate today to what extent Stirner, this unperson from *Vormärz* times, remained an—albeit well-known—obscure figure after the 1848 watershed, or whether he was really widely forgotten or repressed; or whether that contemporary author who expressed his surprise in 1877 that Stirner was so consistently kept out of public discussion, indeed "secreted", was an isolated case.[15]

....

15 Robert Otto Anhuth: *Das wahnsinnige Bewusstsein und die*

Indeed, it seems Stirner was not completely lost in the private sphere; this is evidenced by some important intellectual biographies of the time, such as Eduard von Hartmann's or Friedrich Nietzsche's, but also by the way in which the few mentions are formulated. For example, Friedrich A. Lange in his *Geschichte des Materialismus* (History of Materialism) (1865) evidently assumes *Der Einzige* is not unknown to the reader. However, he dispatches the book, "the most extreme we know at all," assuming the reader's tacit agreement, with a few sentences as an uninteresting side issue.[16] Other individual voices articulated themselves in the same pattern: superlative but brief and evasive.

It is therefore difficult to determine today how strong the real interest in Stirner still was in those decades. However, it can be assumed that the first edition of *Der Einzige*, diminished by confiscations, was widely circulated after 1848. And it is certain that Otto Wigand did not organize a new edition of the book during his lifetime, that is, until 1870. But even from this, no reliable conclusion can be drawn, because Wigand, who was personally very close to Feuerbach, may not have made this decision for commercial reasons.

unbewusste Vorstellung (The Mad Consciousness and the Unconscious Idea). Halle: Fricke, 1877, pp. 521–525.

16   Friedrich Albert Lange: *Geschichte des Materialismus* (History of Materialism) Frankfurt: Suhrkamp 1974. Book II, p. 52.

A second edition of *Der Einzige* was not published until after Otto Wigand's death, by the same publisher, now run by his sons. The reason for this 1882 edition, in which, probably for well-meaning but incomprehensible reasons, the ironic dedication of Stirner to his "sweetheart" was omitted, but no other changes or editorial additions were printed, has not yet been determined. However, a striking indication is that in the same year, at the same publisher, the "Critical Writings" of the brothers Heinrich and Julius Hart appeared, the first combative publication of a new, young, and rebellious generation of poets and writers, an organ of the advancing literary tendency towards realism or naturalism, to which the later Stirner biographer John Henry Mackay can also be attributed.

However, this new edition seems to have hardly generated any public resonance, neither among those who could still remember the first edition and the reactions to it, nor among the young naturalistic avant-garde. To this day, not even a review from the 1880s has become known.

The reasons for the silence of the young generation of writers, which ran counter to publishing expectations, cannot be proven, only speculated. An explanation that could be representative at least for this group can be derived from an autobiographical fragment by the Silesian poet Georg Keben (1859-?), who reports that when he was confronted with Stirner's book as a young man, he was "*im Innersten ergriffen*" (deeply moved) by it, and "*der Zynismus des 'Einzigen' meine ganze jugend-frische Entrüstung heraus[gefordert]*" (the cynicism of *Der Einzige* called forth all my youthful indignation), etc. However, at that time Keben apparently did not articulate his feelings. And a few years later, when he remembered them in an essay about his poet colleague Mackay, they had already faded for him into autobiographical data, because in the meantime Keben had come up with a banal interpretation of Stirner: He now believed that Stirner offered nothing more than "the logical justification of the existing conditions."[17]

A similar reckoning of Stirner can be reconstructed in the case of Hermann Conradi (1862-1890), who belonged to the aforementioned group of literary rebels and, along with the young Mackay, is considered their most radical representative. Usually only indirect traces of that generation's other natiuralists' encounters with Stirner's *Der Einzige* can be found. Mackay, however, took a different path: he openly identified with Stirner's

17 Georg Keben: "Mackay und sein Philosoph" (Mackay and His Philosopher), In: *Monatsblätter. Organ der Breslauer Dichterschule* (Monthly Pages. Organ of the Breslau School of Poetry) 16, 12 (1890), pp. 172–174, 189–190 (190).

ideas and publicly advocated for his work from 1889 until his death in 1933.[18]

The second edition of *Der Einzige* from 1882, which probably did not exceed 1,000 copies, cannot yet be considered the beginning of the first Stirner Renaissance, but it prepared it in the underground. The sale of the book was very difficult since the press ignored it. When Mackay inquired with the publisher in mid-1889 whether a third edition was planned, he received the reply that such a project was "out of the question."[19] Even in 1892, ten years after the publication of the second edition, the head of the Wigand publishing house was of the opinion that "the sales of Stirner's book are unlikely to improve. The community of Stirner is very small, the work was not supported by the press, and my efforts in this direction have been unsuccessful."[20]

This assessment would soon prove to be completely

18   Mackay gave an account of his first encounter with Stirner's *Der Einzige* that, due to his close relationship with Conradi, may be doubted. For a more detailed discussion, see: Bernd A. Laska, "The Difficult Stirner," as well as his "A Lasting Dissident."

19   Letter from Wigand Verlag to John Henry Mackay, dated August 21, 1889. Original in the Mackay estate, archive of the former Institute for Marxism-Leninism, Moscow, Vol. 17.

20   According to information from the publisher Philipp Reclam Jr., Stuttgart, in a letter dated October 28, 1993, to Jochen Knoblauch of the *Archiv für Individualanarchie* (Archive for Individual Anarchy), Berlin. All further information on edition sizes of the Reclam *Der Einzige* taken from this source.

wrong. Despite stagnating sales, the rather subterranean, smoldering effect of the second edition of *Der Einzige* eventually led to several publications in the years 1891–'92 that both indicated and promoted a growing interest in Stirner. The former non-person was suddenly spirited out of oblivion with verve and either "exposed as a precursor to Nietzsche" (e.g. by Eduard von Hartmann) or as a "forerunner of anarchism" (e.g. by Friedrich Engels). However, these genealogies were launched with defamatory intent—which the general public, not just the affected Nietzscheans and anarchists, quickly saw through. Although the discussions about Stirner this triggered remained superficial, they at least temporarily generated a greatly increased interest in his "infamous" book.

In this situation, a new edition of *Der Einzige* was published at the beginning of 1893 in the inexpensive format of Reclam's Universal Library (Nos. 3057-3060), with an astonishing print run of 10,000 copies.[21]

The prehistory of this edition, which proved to be quite lucrative for the Reclam publishing house, is worth a closer look. Because just at that time, when Wigand saw no future for *Der Einzige*, an until then unknown writer

....

21 According to information from the publisher Philipp Reclam Jr., Stuttgart, in a letter dated October 28, 1993, to Jochen Knoblauch of the *Archiv für Individualanarchie* (Archive for Individual Anarchy), Berlin. All further information on edition sizes of the Reclam Einzige taken from this source.

named Paul Lauterbach did not hesitate to make every effort to convince the management of Reclam of the opposite.[22] In the summer of 1892, he achieved his goal: he was entrusted by the Reclam publishing house with the edition of Stirner's *Der Einzige.* Lauterbach therefore turned to Mackay, who was already known as Stirner's future biographer, with a request for biographical data on Stirner for an introduction. Mackay, who saw himself as the true "rediscoverer of Stirner"—and therefore considered Lauterbach, whom he personally did not know, as a rival—coolly ignored this request. Lauterbach's introduction to *Der Einzige* thus clearly shows how little was known about Stirner's life before Mackay's biography of Stirner (1898) was published.

Paul Lauterbach (1860-1895) was one of those brilliant young men who were typical of the *fin de siècle.* He had trained as a chemist at the Fresenius laboratory in Wiesbaden and then studied chemistry (and philosophy) for several semesters in Zurich, but apparently did not aspire to a bourgeois career, as he soon went on extensive travels. He stayed in many countries and returned with profound knowledge in a number of languages, which he used in various literary works. However, as he soon married a young widow with three children and thus had

---

22　Letter from Lauterbach to Mackay, dated June 22, 1892. Original in the Mackay estate, ibid., letters 3 N 18–54.

a family to support, he settled in the book metropolis of Leipzig at the end of the 1880s to establish himself in the publishing industry. Here he worked for, among others, the Reclam publishing house.

Lauterbach was also among the first to adopt Nietzscheanism, probably due to the influence of his friend Heinrich Köselitz alias Peter Gast, who had been a kind of secretary to Nietzsche for many years. He visited the Nietzsche Archive of Elisabeth Förster-Nietzsche and, as a thank you for his commitment to Nietzsche's work, had the privilege of seeing the silent Nietzsche.

At first, the enthusiastic Nietzschean Lauterbach's use of Stirner for his revival may seem strange, since, as mentioned earlier, the much-read and influential philosopher Eduard von Hartmann had just begun to use Stirner against Nietzsche. Hartmann cited the infamous *Der Einzige* to then claim that "Nietzsche's 'New Morality'" was "by no means something new, but had already been presented by Max Stirner in 1845 ... in a masterful form with a clarity and openness that leaves nothing to be desired."[23] Hartmann's intention was clear: he did not want to rehabilitate Stirner, no, he wanted to expose, disgrace, and point out the groundless

....

23   Eduard von Hartmann: "Nietzsches 'neue Moral' (Nietzsche's "New Morality"), in: *Preussische Jahrbücher* (Prussian Yearbook), 67, 5 (1891), p. 504–521 (521).

wickedness of a doctrine that Nietzsche had cleverly hidden behind seductive façades, but that was exposed in all its nudity in Stirner. Hartmann expected the disgust that he assumed to be a normal reaction to *Der Einzige* to be transferred to Nietzsche.

In principle, Lauterbach shared Hartmann's judgment of Stirner. Like Hartmann, he sees that Stirner has laid bare "the deepest root of evil," calls Stirner the "Anti-Geist",[24] and therefore gives him "urgent ethical relevance" as well as an eminent political significance.[25] Lauterbach and Hartmann demonized Stirner as the diabolus of philosophy, but at times they seemed to believe that he was an—extremely clever and meritorious—*advocatus diaboli*. Therefore, both showed the same ambivalent admiration for Stirner's, as they saw it, unique courage in consistency and clarity in the points mentioned.

But Lauterbach's relationship with Nietzsche was opposite to Hartmann's, and therefore, his advocacy for Stirner was pursued with an opposing intention. Lauterbach did not want to demonstrate, like Hartmann, that Nietzsche was little more than a language-manipulating plagiarist. On the contrary, he wanted to present

....

24 "Geist" being the term Stirner used for unchallenged beliefs, sometimes translated as "spirit" or "spook"—UoE.

25 Lauterbach's quotations are taken either from the 8-page introduction to Einzige or, if marked with a date, from his letters to Peter Gast (Gast estate in the Goethe and Schiller Archive, Weimar).

Nietzsche as the only true conqueror, as the "great successor, developer, and [above all] transformer" of Stirner.

Of course, the question arises as to why Lauterbach made such efforts to make *Der Einzige* known, which until then remained almost lost and thus unnecessary to confront. His motives were certainly ambivalent and would be better reconstructed in the context of a comprehensive history of the book's impact. However, it should be noted at this point that, as will be shown later, a comparable ambivalence was decisive for the initiator of the second Stirner Renaissance in the 1960s.

One of his reasons for bringing *Der Einzige* to light, perhaps the most important one, Lauterbach himself expresses in a letter: "My preface has the sole purpose of protecting the innocent from him and mystifying the malicious, paralyzing them, essentially with Nietzsche's help." (February 21, 1893) So, if *Der Einzige* was already on the verge of rediscovery, as he assumed, then an introduction should protect readers from misunderstanding and the public at large from harm caused by the "misuse" of the dangerous text.

Lauterbach acted apparently due to his own, literally painful experience. His past internal struggles against Stirner had resurfaced when he took up *Der Einzige* again for the introduction and only with great effort was able to let it go: "St[irner] tormented me so much last summer that I have copied him 3/4 of the way. What a ferment!" he wrote afterwards to his friend Peter Gast (February 21, 1893). His former and current rescuer in this anxious situation was Nietzsche, and he should also protect future readers of *Der Einzige* from temptations and suffering.

The unsuspecting reader of the introduction, which was included in a total of 84,000 copies from 1893 to 1922, will usually not have perceived the concerned zeal behind it, will not have realized that, as Lauterbach wrote to Gast, "pretty much every word in the introduction is calculated" (April 24, 1893). He would also have hardly understood Lauterbach's secret concern about whether his message would have the desired effect. For much faster than Lauterbach expected and without serious controversies, the self-evident view prevailed everywhere that Nietzsche had "sublated"[26] Stirner in every respect. The question of whether Nietzsche had known Stirner, whom he never mentioned, or not, was of little interest and had no consequences for the evaluation of both thinkers. The Stirner supporters feared the confrontation with Nietzsche's thoughts, which were often greeted euphorically by a large audience. Thus, there was

....

26 "Sublated" is a term used in philosophy that refers to the process of transcending or reconciling a contradiction, where a previously existing idea or concept is negated, but also preserved and lifted up to a higher level of understanding or synthesis.—UoE.

no one who argued offensively with (and for!) Stirner against Nietzsche.

One complementary intention of Lauterbach was to pave the way for Nietzsche, who had not yet achieved fame in 1892, by stylizing him as the saving conqueror of Stirner (who was supposed to form the dark background against which Nietzsche would shine particularly brightly) into the high-selling and affordable Universal Library of Reclam, and thus to a broad readership. His preface should therefore, in addition to protecting "innocents" and paralyzing "malicious" readers, primarily serve the function of "winning Nietzsche readers."

This intention apparently did not correspond with the ideas of the Reclam publishing house, as can be seen from a letter from Lauterbach to Gast: "The introduction is a struggle. Everything original was forbidden. Some contraband was nevertheless saved. The main thing: Nietzsche is in the 'Univ. Bibl.' no matter how concise it may be."

Lauterbach saw his commitment to Nietzsche (and, depending on it, involuntarily also to Stirner) as a (cultural-)political mission. After it became clear that the Reclam *Der Einzige* promised to be a bookselling success, he wrote to Gast with great joy: "*Was ha-ben Stirner und Nietzsche für eine* politische *Rolle zu spie len! Ich wette, dass diesmal Reclam Naumann ins Schlepptau nimmt.*"

(What a *political* role Stirner and Nietzsche have to play! I bet that this time Reclam will take Naumann [the publisher of Nietzsche] in tow).

Paul Lauterbach died on March 24, 1895, and thus did not experience the outcome of the literary project he had so passionately pursued. The triumphant victory he had hoped for of Nietzsche's philosophy formed without the involvement of the Reclam publishing house. The Stirner renaissance he initiated as its vehicle hardly had any effect to this end or philosophical consequences.

The publishing house Otto Wigand released a well-printed third edition of *Der Einzige und sein Eigentum* in 1901 (not counting the Reclam editions that were published in the meantime), but soon realized that this had been an unfortunate decision for the second time. Richard Küster, a grandson of the founder of the publishing house, Otto Wigand, who now ran the company, stated in a letter to John Henry Mackay in 1906, five years after the publication of the book, that "I have not made any money with this book so far, as the reprints [by Reclam] are bought more than my original work." A 62-page brochure on "Max Stirners Lehre" (Max Stirner's Doctrine) by A. Martin, which was published by Wigand in the Stirner anniversary year of 1906 to promote sales, was "only sparsely demanded by the trade booksellers." Küster concluded: "The interest in

Stirner seems to be in decline."[27]

Despite this discouraging news and the strong decline of interest in Stirner as stated in the annual literary reports, which was also evident in the decline of secondary literature, John Henry Mackay realized his long-held desire for a "monumental edition" of *Der Einzige und sein Eigentum* in 1911. He had it printed on "Bütten von van Gelder Zoonen" paper, which bore the signature "John Henry Mackay" as a watermark on each sheet. Mackay believed it was inappropriate to supplement the work with a preface or afterword; he only corrected "some undoubtedly erroneous statements and the printing errors of the original" (which he lists). "The only liberty I have taken," he admits, "is the omission of the dedication." The reasons that prompted him to do so can be found in his Stirner biography.[28]

It is also worth mentioning a failed plan for an edition of *Der Einzige* from 1914. Fritz Mauthner, who wavered in his relationship with Stirner between high and low esteem, like his anarchist friend Gustav Landauer,[29]

27 Letter from Richard Mister (Otto Wigand Company, Leipzig) to John Henry Mackay dated August 30, 1906. Original in the Mackay estate, ibid., F. 307, Nr. 17, L6.

28 Max Stirner: *Der Einzige und sein Eigenthum*, edited by John Henry Mackay. Monumental edition in 980 numbered copies. With a four-page supplement in a slipcase. Charlottenburg, 1911. Self-published, 355 pages, large quarto.

29 See Bernd A. Laska: *Der schwierige Stirner* ("The Difficult Stirner"),

almost included it in the "Library of Philosophers" published by the Munich publisher Georg Müller. This is documented in a letter to the poet and philosopher Erwin Guido Kolbenheyer, who had suggested including the Stirner dissertation of his friend Hermann Schultheiss[30] and possibly Stirner's *Der Einzige* in this series. In it, Mauthner wrote: *"Meine Bewunderung für Stirner, der auch dann noch ein Kerl ist, wo er grotesk wird, ist so stark, dass ich 'prinzipiell' sehr gern bereit bin, ihn vollständig in die Bibl.d.Phil. aufzunehmen"* (My admiration for Stirner, who remains a man even when he becomes grotesque, is so strong that I am 'principally' very willing to include him completely in the Library of Philosophers).[31] Mauthner's plan, however, remained unrealized because the publisher discontinued the book series in 1914.

The sale of the Mackay luxury edition of *Der Einzige* from 1911 was hardly more favorable than the sales of the two previous, well printed Wigand editions from

----

ibid., as well as the same: *Ein dauerhafter Dissident* (A Permanent Dissident), ibid.

30 Hermann Schultheiss: *Stirner. Grundlagen zum Verständnis des Werkes Der Einzige und sein Eigentum* (Foundations for Understanding the Work Der Einzige und sein Eigentum). (PhD thesis, Greifswald 1905). Ratibor: F. Lindner 1906; Second edition edited by Richard Dedo. Leipzig: Felix Meiner, 1922.

31 Letter from Fritz Mauthner to Erwin Guido Kolbenheyer dated April 23, 1914; original in the Kolbenheyer Archive, Geretsried.

1882 and 1901. Stirner's book was apparently only sellable in cheap editions—an editorial-historical fact that, incidentally, was repeated in the second Stirner renaissance from 1968 and deserves attention, especially in the context of the social impact of the book.

Another equally remarkable and not easily explainable fact of editorial history is that at a time when Stirner was hardly discussed publicly, the sales of the Reclam edition of *Der Einzige* actually increased significantly. Following the first edition of 10,000 in 1893, which was already remarkably high for a supposedly specialized philosophical book, editions of 5,000 copies were published in the years of Stirner's popularity, i.e., 1897, 1900, 1903, and 1905. The sales of the last edition can be explained by the publicity surrounding Stirner's 100th birthday and 50th anniversary of his death in 1906. However, the numbers for the years that followed are difficult to explain: 5,000 copies were published in 1907, 10,000 copies in both 1908 and 1912, 13,000 copies in 1913, and another 8,000 copies in 1919 and 1922. The last edition of the first Stirner renaissance was printed in 1927 and consisted of 5,000 copies.

Roughly calculated, this means an annual sales figure of 2,500 for the period from 1893 to the "Stirner year" of 1906, and almost 4,000 copies for a roughly equivalent period thereafter. It wasn't until the 1920s that sales figures rapidly declined. From then until the end of the 1960s, approximately four decades later, the book was largely forgotten again.

Except for the last edition, all of these volumes, a total of 84,000 copies, were provided with Lauterbach's introduction. Since it was intended to lead to Nietzsche rather than Stirner, it was actually an objective annoyance, but it was hardly perceived as such. Anyone who wanted to persuade the publisher to commission a new introduction would have needed a precise understanding of Stirner's singular philosophical position—and the courage to confront the widely adored Nietzsche with the unpopular Stirner. John Henry Mackay, however, the only advocate of Stirner, declared himself incompetent in this regard ("I am not a philosopher..."[32]) and only objected to Lauterbach's text as follows: "The arbitrary use of all sorts of 'related' thinkers and the uncritical quotations from their works can only do more harm than good, and the resulting confusion is all the more regrettable, since this edition will probably remain the most accessible to wider circles for a long time. Moreover, the pompous and affected style is in the most unpleasant contrast to the clear, chiseled language of the work itself." He added the following sentence to this remark, which

....
32   In the preface to the second edition (1910) of his Stirner biography, reprinted in the third edition, p. XIII.

33

appears in the introduction to Mackay's first Stirner biography from 1898: "I am therefore pleased that I will be allowed to replace this introduction with another, my own, in a new edition."[33]

Mackay had already complained about Lauterbach's introduction at Reclam for years,[34] but in 1910 he was told that they wanted to resolve the matter with Lauterbach, whose death in 1895 neither the publisher nor Mackay apparently knew about. It was not until 1927, as he writes in his "Reckoning," that Mackay was able to replace the "impossible preface" with his own. "I attach particular importance to this brief summary," he said.[35] Mackay's preface was now "impossible" in its own way: inadequate due to its hagiographic passages and, in terms of its lack of color and strength, far less interesting than Lauterbach's. In terms of content, he contented himself with a pale summary of biography and book, avoiding any confrontation with the failed, consistently evasive reception.

For the sake of completeness, it should be mentioned that in the 1920s, in addition to the Reclam volumes, several other editions of *Der Einzige* were published

....

33   John Henry Mackay: *Max Stirner - sein Leben und sein Werk* (Max Stirner: His Life and Work). Third edition 1914 (reprint 1977), p. 20.

34   Since March 1, 1910, as evidenced by a letter from the publisher to Mackay. Original in the Mackay estate, ibid., Letters 3 N 18–54.

35   John Henry Mackay: *Abrechnung* (Reckoning). Berlin-Charlottenburg: Self-published, 1932, p. 84.

in unknown print runs.[36] Their editors, A. Schulze or Anselm Ruest, also preceded Stirner's text with introductions that, like Mackay's, were well-intentioned and attempted to honor the vilified thinker, but largely ignored the actual problems associated with Stirner, such as his potential intellectual rank or the Stirner-Nietzsche question.

All in all, therefore, over 100,000 copies of Stirner's *Der Einzige* were sold in the four decades from 1890 to 1930. As a book of its genre, it was undoubtedly a "hit," at least in commercial terms, even if, apart from the few years of increased publicity around 1900, it was rather "secretive." Nevertheless, the official representatives of this genre, the academic philosophers, condemned the work by silently ignoring it.

Nevertheless, for a number of thinkers of that time, including prominent ones such as Edmund Husserl, Carl Schmitt, Rudolf Steiner, and Ludwig Klages, a deeply existential encounter with Stirner's book can be documented, which is all the more interesting as these thinkers, like Marx and Nietzsche before them, avoided a public confrontation with it. These indirect but all the more powerful signals of a perennial relevance of *Der*

....

36 See bibliography in Hans G. Helms: *Die Ideologie der anonymen Gesellschaft* (The Ideology of the Anonymous Society). Cologne: DuMont 1966. pp. 516f.

Einzige have not ceased even today: as mentioned above, for example, Jürgen Habermas apparently had great difficulties in processing Stirner's theses in his early days (see Husseris Politik, not to warn against Stirner at all).[37] Despite its nominal level of recognition and the accumulation of often more journalistic secondary literature, Stirner's *Der Einzige* can also be described as a hit in that other sense briefly explained at the beginning—and in this sense, even more so as a "secretive" one.

The so-called Stirner Renaissance, which began almost unnoticed in the 1880s and suddenly gained momentum with the publication of the Lauterbach Reclam edition of *Der Einzige* in early 1893, had already reached its peak in the Stirner Year of 1906 and subsided until the 1920s. It could be called the first, because a second followed.

The beginnings of the second Stirner Renaissance, which date back to the 1960s, show at least two fundamental parallels to those of the first: a contemporary and a personal one.

Firstly, there were also about four decades prior, during which no opportunity existed for the interest in the problems raised by Stirner to grow, after it had to

37   See also footnotes 1 and 2.

give way to pressing (daily) political issues in the after-math of a turbulent period (1848 or 1933). Then, once again, it was an intellectual-political movement, such as the naturalist movement of the 1880s, which creat-ed the conditions for the revival of interest in Stirner at all: the student movement of the 1960s. And, like the naturalist movement, it only had a catalytic function for the renewed Stirner Renaissance: *Der Einzige* was and remained irrelevant to their theoretical debates, and Stirner was at best a meaningless peripheral figure, known only by name in connection with Marx.

If one sees Paul Lauterbach as the man who, with his committed efforts for the Reclam edition of *Der Einzige* in 1893, gave the decisive impulse to the first Stirner Renaissance as an individual, then a comparable role was played by the writer Hans Günter Helms (born 1932) in the second. The second, personal parallel mentioned above is that both Lauterbach and Helms—a curious fact of edition history—were vehement opponents of the previously little-known author whom they propagat-ed and edited effectively for the first time.

Hans Günter Helms became an opponent of Stirner because, like Lauterbach, he saw *Der Einzige* as the pur-est literary form of what Stirner had called the "deepest root of evil"—but, as a Marxist, he used a different termi-nology than his Nietzschean predecessor. Moreover, as a young man, Helms was deeply disturbed and alarmed by various "right-wing" historical continuities that remained effective in West Germany even after 1945. Both aspects merged more and more in his thinking into a single complex, so that he felt he had a socio-political mission to fulfill with his "anti-fascist" struggle against Stirner, just as Paul Lauterbach had before him.

To contribute to the interruption of those continuities, Helms contacted the Frankfurt "Institute for Social Research" at the end of the 1950s, which had relocated from the USA a few years earlier, first to Max Horkheimer, and then to Theodor Adorno, whom he felt close to because of his musical interests and his love-hate relationship with Heidegger. At that time, Adorno was working on the book about Heidegger, which he then gave the title *Jargon der Eigentlichkeit* (The Jargon of Authenticity) and the subtitle *Zur deutschen Ideologie* (Towards the German Ideology). With the use of some specific interpretive aids, one may discern in it the suggestion that the current confrontation between Adorno and Heidegger corresponds to the former Marx/Stirner conflict—which understandably should not be expressed more clearly.

In any case, it was likely discussions at the institute with external participants Helms and Kurt Mautz (a former Adorno student and Stirner expert)[38] on this topic that gave shape to Helms' subsequent Stirner book, *Die Ideologie der anonymen Gesellschaft* (The Ideology of the Anonymous Society).[39] In it, Helms explicitly thanks Adorno and Horkheimer,[40] but remains silent about the institute's closer involvement. In fact, the institute had initially agreed to publish the book in its own scientifically renowned "Institutsreihe," but later withdrew its commitment under false pretenses.

The true reasons for the institute's distancing from Helms probably had less to do with fundamental substantive disagreements and more to do with tactical considerations. Adorno had praised Stirner as the author who had truly "let the cat out of the bag,"[41] but Helms' zealous and vulgar approach (such as his hasty and unsubstantiated branding of Heidegger as a Stirner epigone)[42] may have seemed too crude, too sensational, and too easily attacked for Adorno to want to be associated with it. Ultimately, the institute probably interpreted Marx's ambiguous behavior towards *Der Einzige*,

....

38   Kurt Mautz: *Die Philosophie Max Stirners im Gegensatz zum Hegelschen Idealismus* (The Philosophy of Max Stirner in Contrast to Hegelian Idealism). Berlin: Junker a Dünnhaupt, 1936.

39   Hans G. Helms: *Die Ideologie...*, op. cit., 620 p.

40   Ibid., p. 502.

41   Cited in Ibid., p. 200.

42   Ibid., throughout, especially pp. 95, 151, 181, 355, 474.

particularly his public reserve, as more correct and intelligent than Helms did, and followed suit. In any case, neither Adorno nor Horkheimer nor any other author associated with or close to the institute ever addressed Stirner. Helms' book was eventually published in 1966 by the Cologne publisher DuMont.

The characterization of Heidegger, undoubtedly intended as a smear, is only one aspect of Helms' work and is highlighted here solely for reasons of its genesis. The list of those whom Helms also ranks as "Stirner apprentices" is long and contains many names of authors who either did not mention or know Stirner, like Heidegger, or who were explicitly opposed to him. On the book cover, Helms even tries to associate figures like Mussolini and Goebbels with Stirner, and in the text, even Hitler. Ultimately, it remains unclear who is supposed to be defamed by this strange procession of affinities, but it is also of little interest.

Helms wrote his book in the name of a universal "anti-fascism" that opposes a similarly universal "fascism". And he believes to have exposed the truest, purest, first, and yet most skillfully disguised arch-ideologues of this fascism, especially of German National Socialism and its democratically disguised continuation in the political system of the Federal Republic—namely Stirner. "Stirner's demagogic techniques," Helms claims, "have not yet been surpassed in modernity and sophistication by any descendant."[43] Therefore, it was historically high time that "Marxists finally took notice of the abscess [Stirner]."[44]

Helms wanted to provide a kind of update to Marx's anti-Stirner "Saint Max" polemic with his Manichean brute construct, a sharp weapon in the ideological struggle. He was right to sense that Marx had once recognized in Stirner his strongest opponent and antipode, but he was unable to interpret Stirner's "not always consistent behavior"[45] as an indication of a fundamental weakness in Marx's position. However, nobody else had tackled this problem either; yet all others who had engaged with the early Marx, no matter how intensely, had sleepwalked around it.[46]

Helms, of course, noticed the evasive attitude of Marxist theorists but interpreted it superficially as an influence of "revisionist" tendencies. With his work, which exceeds the length of Marx's anti-Stirner manuscript, he wanted to rectify or initiate the rectification of this ideological deficit of

43 Hans G. Helms (ed.): *Max Stirner. Der Einzige und sein Eigentum und andere Schriften.* Munich: Hanser, 1968. "Afterword," p. 278.

44 Hans G. Helms: *Die Ideologie...*, op. cit., p. 495.

45 Ibid., p. 502.

46 One notable figure during the time when Helms wrote his book was Louis Althusser (Pour Marx, 1965). This evasive stance was not limited to Marxists. Among the few still half-hearted exceptions is Wolfgang Essbach: *Die Bedeutung Max Stirners...*, op. cit.

Marxism that had developed over decades. However, the reviewers, even the Marxist ones, appreciated this or that aspect of the work, criticized and praised, but generally, with ambivalent consideration for the engaged anti-fascist author, silently passed over his actual concern. They simply didn't understand why someone would first elevate the long-forgotten Stirner in a monomaniacal way and then destroy him with almost absurd means.

It took Helms several years until he realized the futility of his ambitious project and silently retreated from working on it, shifting his focus to peripheral journalistic areas. However, before doing so, the Hanser-Verlag had commissioned him to edit a selection of Stirner's works for a paperback series. (Helms might have hoped that understanding the text his work, *The Ideology of the Anonymous Society*, was directed against—would be better achieved by knowing the text itself.) Through this edition, even though heavily abridged, *Der Einzige* returned to the market after more than forty years, making Helms, perhaps unwillingly, the initiator of the second Stirner Renaissance. Nonetheless, this renaissance did not yield the expected impact, much like the first one initiated by Lauterbach.

At first, it seems astonishing that Hanser accepted Helms as the editor, since although he had established himself as an expert in the technical sense through his book, he was also an excessively fanatical opponent of Stirner, who could not refrain from absurd manipulations. Ultimately, a reduction of *Der Einzige* to half its size was planned, thereby creating a significant possibility for tendentious distortion of the original work. In fact, Helms seems to have had largely free rein in the Hanser edition. He engaged in selective fragmentation, which he had previously accused Eduard Bernstein, the first editor of Marx's "Saint Max," of doing in an accusatory manner, in an excessive way: he cut *Der Einzige* into over 80 fragments and put half of them together into a text that he said contained the "central sections." Helms does not provide a description of the principles he used to edit and select the text; instead, he adds an afterword that reveals the basic features of his "anti-fascist" Stirner interpretation from his previous book. The cover does not feature the same promotional statement as Helms' ideological book, which placed Stirner in the company of Goebbels and Mussolini, but it does include the following absurd statement: "The doctrine of the 'Einzige' justifies capitalism and administratively ordered chaos, justifies falsehood and injustice, having and not having, its ideal is unsocial and anonymous existence, and it even justifies murder."

Thus, at Hanser, the goat was put in charge of the garden. One (partial) explanation for this appalling situation is that prominent Marxists, especially the philosopher Hans Heinz Holz, sat on the editorial board of the "Hanser series" in which the mutilated *Der Einzige* appeared. Holz was one of the very few who still considered Stirner to be the "most dangerous" thinker of all time, even during a period when he had largely been forgotten. On the 100th anniversary of Stirner's death, June 25, 1956, Holz therefore warned the world—albeit with less text, but in no less apocalyptic terms than Helms later did—that wherever "Stirner's postulate of egoism is taken seriously, all human existence would cease."[47] It is therefore not surprising that Helms was the right man for Stirner's editor and commentator in Holz's view. Nevertheless, it remains more than astonishing and can only be understood in the context of the many other peculiarities of Stirner's reception that ideological solidarity could blind people to the extent that such blatantly absurd constructs as Helms' could pass all rational checks.

The halved and patched-together *Der Einzige* by van Helms, composed of 40 fragments, appeared at Hanser from 1968 to 1970 in three editions totaling 11,000 copies—a sales success that is on par with that of the 1890s. Helms formulated the afterword entirely in the spirit of his "ideology of anonymous society" and

---

47   Cited in Hans G. Helms: *Die Ideologie...*, op. cit., p. 105.

repeated his most important theses here: Stirner had created "an ideological delusion"; this was "an ideology that reflects quite accurately the misery and vain hopes of the contemporary German petit bourgeois"; it is "the prototype of the prevailing consciousness state here and now in the BRD" (Bundesrepublik Deutschland, or Federal Republic of Germany)." Helms' almost paranoid demonization of Stirner, against which none of the reviewers of his ideological book had uttered a clear word, rages here uncontrollably, for example, when he calls Stirner the greatest demagogue of all time, or when he sees disguised fascists at work everywhere: "The phalanx of open Stirnerians is large, the number of hidden brothers in the unspiritual world is even greater." If one reads Helms' list of named historical Stirnerians, which of course "could only be a small selection," it becomes clear that basically meant everyone who was not a Marxist after 1845: Bakunin, Landauer, and Mühsam as well as (Carl) Schmitt, Dietrich Eckart (a mentor of Hitler's), and Mussolini; Belinski, Turgenjew, and Dostoyevsky as well as Heidegger, Camus, and Sartre—and many more.

This comment, difficult to surpass in its absurdity, which, however, achieved far greater dissemination than Helms' voluminous Stirner book, was apparently received with indifference by the public, including the experts, or judged with the greatest indulgence—as before with the book, as now with the mutilation of *Der Einzige*. In any case, nothing happened that would have prompted the publisher to distance himself from a second and third edition or at least to deliver them without this afterword (or with a different one).

As early as November 7, 1963, the West German Reclam publishing house informed Helms in response to an inquiry that Stirner's *Der Einzige* belonged "among the works of world literature that will one day be available again in an inexpensive edition."[48] Nine years later, in 1972, immediately following the Hanser edition, it happened: *Der Einzige* was published anew and unabridged in Reclam's Universal Library under the old number 3057-3060. The initial print run was 7,500 copies. Four more editions were required before 1991, so that from 1972 to today, approximately 28,000 copies have been printed. Although these numbers fall short of those of the first Stirner Renaissance, they are still remarkable, considering the subject matter and, above all, the reputation of the book.

The new Reclam edition of *Der Einzige und sein Eigentum* had a new editor who wrote a new afterword. It must remain open here on what criteria the new editor was selected; whether perhaps the expert Helms was not commissioned only because he had already been

---

48   Cited in Hans G. Helms: *Die Ideologie...*, op. cit., p.17.

responsible for the Hanser edition shortly before, or because he was no longer available. In any case, apparently Reclam also had no reservations about an editor who feels particularly committed to Marx and the worldview he founded: neither from the simple consideration that with the specific author Stirner, against whom Marx wrote the most elaborate of his philosophical treatises, a Marxist could have particular problems, nor from the experience of the fiasco with Helms—which, however, as noted above, was mostly not even perceived as such. For they chose Ahlrich Meyer, a young political scientist who had already made a name for himself with Marxist-oriented publications.

Now, in his 39-page afterword, Meyer does not explicitly follow Helms, but he spares him, even though a clear word would have been necessary regarding both his Stirner pastiche and his widely known Stirner commentaries. Meyer remains relatively disciplined in his lecture, although he believes he must expose the "trick of all Stirner apologetics"[49] right at the beginning. His historical expertise and scientific jargon do the rest suggesting to the reader, who is usually not familiar with the subtleties of Stirner's ideas' reception and interpretation, that this afterword is predominantly an informative aid

....

49   Meyer deleted this sentence at the beginning of his introduction in 1981.

to reading—although a critical reader of the (unnecessarily) supplied interpretation would of course have to recognize its ideological background.

Meyer's aversion to the author he edited only becomes apparent in a postscript "On the 1981 Reissue," which he believed he had to add to his afterword for the fourteenth through eighteen thousandth copies (since the publisher did not allow a new version of the afterword?). Therein, he laments—as the editor!—first "the necessity of a new reprint." Unfortunately, "the intellectual misery of its [*Der Einzige und sein Eigentum*] origin" still has not been recognized. As a result, "the renaissance of anti-Marxist thought and various existentialist ghetto ideologies" have brought new successes to the terrible book. One can probably suspect Helms's fantasies in the background, when Meyer notes with great concern, "that we are not yet done with Stirner."

Apart from Meyer's deep aversion towards Stirner, whom he attempted to present, as far as possible, as isolated from, in isolation from his other social history, in this work, also attempted to present the editorial history of Max Stirner's book *Der Einzige und sein Eigentum.* Peripheral aspects were consciously ignored because the aim was to clearly highlight the peculiarity of this history.[50] The revivals of Stirner's book in 1893 and 1968,

....

50 A secondary aspect might be, for instance, the chronology of foreign-

which brought the book back into relatively high circu-
lation after it had been completely forgotten, were the
result of the dedicated efforts of one person each: Paul
Lauterbach in 1893 and Hans Günter Helms in 1968.
Both were convinced, apparently due to a strong, albeit
negative intuition, of the extraordinary intellectual significance of Stirner. Both saw, probably through empa-
thetic understanding of the intellectual biography of the
thinker whom they each revered as superior to all others
(Nietzsche or Marx), Stirner as the epitome of the (evil)
principle to be fought against.[51] However, in their ador-
ing attitudes, they were so blinded that they did not recognize the tactical finesse, the unconscious calculations

....

language edition of *Der Einzige.* Another more intriguing secondary aspect might be to closely examine the reasons why Stirner's *Der
Einzige*, which is repeatedly considered a cornerstone of anarchism,
never saw publication by an anarchist publishing house.

51 For Helms, the matter was clear, as Marx's anti-Stirner work "Saint
Max" had been available since 1932. However, for Lauterbach, it
was clear that Nietzsche knew Stirner, even without a comparable
text. On September 18, 1892, he wrote to Gast: "*Unter uns gesagt:
er [Nietzsche] muss St[irner] gekannt haben. Aber das Verhältnis ist
ein kompliziertes.*" (Between us: he [Nietzsche] must have known
St[irner]. But the relationship is complicated.) Since there was no ev-
idence for this claim at that time, and Lauterbach's friend Peter Gast,
who had been in close contact with Nietzsche for years, was of a different opinion, Lauterbach noted in a footnote to his introduction that
Nietzsche probably did not know Stirner.

For the latter problem, see Bernd A. Laska: *Neues Licht auf die
Stirner-Nietzsche-Frage*, op. cit.

with which these successful philosophers kept Stirner away from themselves and the world. As a result, both were absolutely sure that their respective heroes had already won the necessary, decisive victory over Stirner. Therefore, both wanted to present Stirner, who had long been forgotten, to highlight the greatness of their masters' deeds. Both wanted to "prove" that Nietzsche or Marx was the thinker with whose help the impending catastrophe could be most effectively averted, because both understood their actions as eminently political.

Strangely enough, Stirner, who was twice brought out of obscurity into public consciousness by philosophical "amateurs" due to a perhaps paradoxical motive and against the ideologically cautious gatekeepers, did not have the devastating effect all those who suppressed, vilified, silenced, or feared him had feared. Stirner became a bestselling, often admired, but rarely discussed author each time. However, this had hardly any consequences, because ultimately he remained a footnote to Marx and/or Nietzsche, who styled themselves as "great thinkers. A serious reception of *Der Einzige und sein Eigentum*, without an understanding of the evasive the evasive maneuvers of the greats in the face of the problems raised by Stirner, still faces powerful obstacles, despite the dwindling prestige of those thinkers.

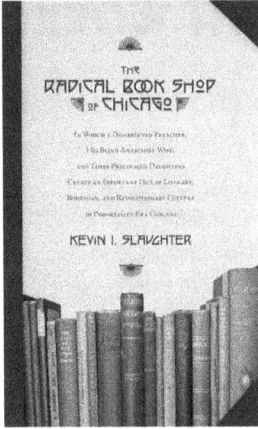

The Radical Book Shop of Chicago:
In Which a Disaffected Preacher, His Blind
Anarchist Wife, and Their Precocious
Daughters Create an Important Hub of Literary,
Bohemian, and Revolutionary Culture in
Progressive-Era Chicago
Kevin I. Slaughter, with appendix by Lillian Undell
130 pages, 6x9",
ISBN 978-1943687282

A Brave and Beautiful Spirit:
Dora Marsden, 1882-1960
Les Garner
6×9", 486 pages
ISBN-13: 978-1944651145

Hyde Park Orator Illustrated
Bonar Thompson
Trevor Blake (introduction)
6×9", 354 pages
ISBN-13: 978-1944651183

WWW.UNIONOFEGOISTS.COM

STANDARD FREETHOUGHT WORKS

CONFESSIONS OF A FAILED EGOIST—*Trevor Blake*.................. $10
ELBERT HUBBARD'S THE PHILISTINE—*Bruce A. White*.................. $16
HOMO 99 AND 44/100 NONSAPIENS—*Gerald B. Lorentz* $18
MIGHT IS RIGHT: THE AUTHORTITATIVE EDITION—*Ragnar Redbeard*...... $20
MIGHT IS RIGHT: 1927 FACSIMILE EDITION—*Ragnar Redbeard*.......... $16
THE OCCULT TECHNOLOGY OF POWER—*The Transcriber*............... $8
THE PHILOSOPHICAL WRITINGS OF EDGAR SALTUS—*Edgar Saltus* $18
THE RADICAL BOOK SHOP OF CHICAGO—*Kevin I. Slaughter*........... $16
RIVAL CAESARS: A ROMANCE...—*Ragnar Redbeard* $20
THE SATANIC SCRIPTURES—*Peter H. Gilmore*........................$17
SORCERIES AND SCANDALS OF SATAN—*Henry M. Tichenor* $15
THIS UGLY CIVILIZATION—*Ralph Borsodi*.......................... $20

BENJAMIN DeCASSERES SERIES:
ANATHEMA! LITANIES OF NEGATION $10
FANTASIA IMPROMPTU & FINIS................................ $16
FULMINATIONS: CAUSTIC, COSMIC, CAPRICIOUS $16
IMP: THE POETRY OF BENJAMIN DeCASSERES $15
NEW YORK IS HELL: THINKING AND DRINKING IN THE BEAUTIFUL BEAST .. $18
SPINOZA: LIBERATOR OF GOD AND MAN & AGAINST THE RABBIS $15
THE BOY OF BETHLEHEM—*Bio DeCasseres* (Hardbound)............... $23
THE SUBLIME BOY—*Walter DeCasseres*........................... $7

THE PORTABLE L.A.ROLLINS SERIES:
THE MYTH OF NATURAL RIGHTS................................ $15
LUCIFER'S LEXICON $15
OUTLAW HISTORY $15
DISJECTA MEMBRA ....(coming soon)

PAMPHLETS

BOVARYSM: THE ART-PHILOSOPHY OF JULES DE GAULTIER—*Wilmot E. Ellis* .. $4
IMMORALITY AS A PHILOSOPHIC PRINCIPLE—*Paul Carus* $5
MAX STIRNER AND THE PHILOSOPHY OF THE INDIVIDUAL—*Leo Markun* ... $8
MAN-EATING AND MAN-SACRIFICING—*Anon*........................ $3
THE NIETZSCHE MOVEMENT IN ENGLAND—*Oscar Levy* $2
PRIMITIVES: POEMS AND WOODCUTS—*Max Weber* $6

UNDERWORLD AMUSEMENTS
444 MARYLAND AVE. #7940   ESSEX, MD 21221
For postage add $4 for the first item, $1 for each additional.
Or visit WWW.UNDERWORLDAMUSEMENTS.COM

www.ingramcontent.com/pod-product-compliance
Lightning Source LLC
Chambersburg PA
CBHW060259030426
42335CB00014B/1771